A SEASON OF FLOWERS

"Earth laughs in flowers."
—Ralph Waldo Emerson

Tilbury House Publishers
12 Starr Street
Thomaston, Maine 04861
800-582-1899 • www.tilburyhouse.com

Hardcover ISBN 978-088448-623-7
eBook ISBN 978-9-88448-625-1

First hardcover printing December 2017

15 16 17 18 19 20 XXX 10 9 8 7 6 5 4 3 2 1

Library of Congress Control Number: 2017953867

Cover and interior designed by Frame25 Productions
Printed in Korea through Four Colour Print Group, Louisville, KY

To Master Gardeners Al and
Dimmy Lotricchiano, with
grateful thanks for their
review of the book.

A SEASON OF
FLOWERS
MICHAEL GARLAND

TILBURY HOUSE PUBLISHERS
THOMASTON, MAINE

Snowdrop and Crocus

We are the earliest flowers of spring.
Robins devour the bugs that we bring.

Tulip and Hyacinth
A feast for rabbits, row upon row,
vibrant and bright, we're next in the show.

Dogwood

White or pink blossoms make me the best.
My branches provide a safe place for a nest.

Moths come to feed in the dim twilight hour.
My sweetness makes me their chosen flower.

Lupine

My blossoms spread color on fields by the bunch;
the nectar within is a hummingbird's lunch.

Daisy

When summer heats up, I'm next to arrive.
My scent in the air brings bees from their hives.

Morning Glory

My beautiful blooms have such a brief stay!
They open in morning and last just a day.

Daylily

I stand tall and proud by the old garden wall,
until nibbling deer leave nothing at all.

Native Geranium

A chipmunk finds food and does some good deeds.
I can grow wild when he spreads my seeds.

Peony

I'm high on the list of beautiful plants.
If you take me indoors, check first for ants.

Sunflower

I turn toward the sun, heavy with seed.
Birds drop by to perch and to feed.

Rose

Beetles love roses, everyone warns.
Nothing will stop them, not even my thorns.

Chrysanthemums

The days have grown shorter; autumn is here.
Hold on to summer by keeping me near.

Now we slumber and wait for rebirth.
We are nature's great gift to the earth.

THE SEASON OF FLOWERS

Without bright, colorful flowers, the world would be a lot less beautiful and fragrant than it is.

A flower has male parts that produce pollen and female parts that produce egg cells. When grains of pollen fertilize egg cells, the flower develops into a fruit containing seeds, and each seed can sprout into a new plant. Flowers use fragrance and bright colors to attract the insects that spread their pollen. When a bee carries pollen from one clover blossom to another, it is helping the clover to reproduce. In return for this **pollination**, the bee gets pollen and nectar to take back to its hive. And when birds, chipmunks, squirrels, and other animals carry seeds to their nests or store them for later eating, they drop a few that sprout, spreading the plant to new locations. Everyone benefits, and it has been going on like this since flowering plants evolved some 200 million years ago.

Each year, like magic, flowers bloom again in their accustomed months. Some flowering plants are **annuals**, which means they die each autumn and are replaced from seeds the following year. Some are **perennials**, which means that the plant's roots survive the winter and put out new growth in the spring. And some flowers are perennials in one climate and annuals in another.

In much of North America, the season of flowers begins in early spring and lasts until late autumn, and you can follow the passage of time by observing which flowers are in bloom. There are many, many flowers besides the ones in this book. Learning to recognize them is one of the joys of being outdoors and a key to appreciating the play of nature.

The flowers in this book appear roughly in order of their blooming. Most of them, however, have multiple species and varieties with different bloom times.

Snowdrops and **crocuses** are among the earliest flowers. Snowdrops appear as early as January in mild climates or as late as late March in cold areas, and crocuses follow soon after. Small and delicate, these perennials provide pollen and nectar for bees coming out of hibernation. They are nature's promise that winter is ending.

Tulips are tall perennials with one flower on each stem. **Hyacinths** are short, stout plants with many little blossoms on a stem. Hyacinths are perennials wherever the winters are cold enough to chill the bulbs and prepare the plants to bloom again.

Dogwoods are flowering trees that bloom between March and June, depending on where you live. The blossoms of various species are pink or white. Dogwood branches buzz with insects and make fine nesting sites for birds. The berries that appear in the summer nourish baby birds. The blossoming of dogwoods was once a sign to Native Americans that it was time to plant corn.

Iris is a tall perennial that blooms in late spring. The many varieties of irises have pink, blue, red, yellow, or purple flowers. Vincent van Gogh and many other artists have painted irises. When moths flutter over iris blossoms on mild evenings, they unfurl their long tongues to dip into the flowers' nectar.

Lupine is a perennial that blooms from early to midsummer in a garden or in the wild. Lupines come in a range of colors: pink, white, rust, red, orange, blue, and violet.

Daisies can be found on every continent except Antarctica. Larger white or yellow petals surround a disc, or "eye," of smaller yellow petals. The perfume of a daisy is irresistible to bees.

The **morning glory** is a vine with beautiful flowers that bloom in a single day, appearing early in the morning and fading as the day goes by. Though usually an annual, some varieties of morning glory will grow as a perennial in mild climates.

Daylilies are perennials. A daylily flower lasts no more than twenty-four hours. Deer eat daylilies as if they were candy.

Wild geraniums have five petals and a variety of colors, including red, pink, white, and blue. Geranium seedpods burst when dry, flinging seeds outward and helping the plants spread even when there are no chipmunks around to scatter the seeds.

Grown all over the world, **peonies** have been a longtime inspiration in traditional Asian art. Their sweet nectar is a magnet for ants. Plump, showy, and beautiful, these perennials blossom in high summer.

Sunflowers have a large head that turns to follow the sun's arc across the sky. The petals of these annuals are red, yellow, and orange. A sunflower produces many seeds in late summer, which can be eaten or planted to grow new sunflowers. Sunflowers were another favorite subject in Vincent van Gogh's paintings.

A **rose** is a woody perennial shrub. Roses are the most celebrated of flowers and have been cultivated into more varieties than any other. The flowers range in size from small to large and in color from white or yellow to red. The thorns of roses protect them from many animals, but not from insects. Japanese beetles love to feast on roses. From mid spring into the fall, there are always roses in bloom. Some bloom continuously or repeatedly throughout the season; others flower only once each year, putting on a spectacular display.

Known as "mums" for short, **chrysanthemums** come in a variety of species and in colors from white to rust. They bloom from late summer to early winter, and the later-blooming varieties add color to the landscape when little else is in bloom. The hardier species are perennials, surviving the winter to put forth new growth year after year. These are known as hardy mums.

MICHAEL GARLAND is the author and illustrator of 34 children's picture books and the illustrator of more than 40 books written by others. *Miss Smith and the Haunted Library* is a *New York Times* bestseller. Other recent books include *Daddy Played the Blues*, *Lost Dog, Tugboat, Car Goes Far, Fish Had a Wish* (starred review from *Publisher's Weekly*), *Where's My Homework?*, and *Grandpa's Tractor* (selected for the Original Art of Children's Book Show by the Society of Illustrators in NYC). Michael's *Christmas Magic* has become a seasonal classic. Michael created the illustrations for *A Season of Flowers* using a digital collage technique that he has developed. Michael makes school visits across the country. To learn more, stop by his website, www.garlandpicturebooks.com.